seventeen

writer with an open heart

Seventeen is about a family, dangerously held together by loss and lies, and enduring love.

The narrative is me as I navigate the hills and valleys my family and I experienced with my older brother Craig at the wheel.

Opening with me at eight-years old and the fear that my secret will be discovered by a neighbor who passed away, the reader learns of the abuse I experienced by way of Craig's hands and selfish demands.

And just as time moves forward and lives change, the reader is introduced to the present day, discovering Craig suffered a seizure and is now placed in a coma.

The story flows from present to past, taking the reader on a journey of the Gary family - eventually culminating and sealing Craig's fate.

The namesake *seventeen* is a tribute to my late mother who passed on September 17, 2002. The number 17 has since been an angel number, one of which I see and hear almost annoyingly throughout my day. I even married my husband, Jack on March 17, 2008 – adding to the synchronicity that is my life.

seventeen

This is a book about my life. But it is not a memoir – I do not believe in them. My memories are my memories. They are not my family's nor Craig's. It wouldn't be fair to say that my experience was their own.

I have aired the proverbial closet in this soul-revealing novella. For that, I've changed the names of all involved to protect the guilty.

My hope for sharing my story is to explain my idiosyncrasies and the bruises I carry like armor – both for the reader and myself. And to share in your pain because I know families are messy, love is innately painful yet beautiful, and life is not always linear.

I believe that we all have experienced something that has changed us forever and for that, we all deserve compassion and love. Telling my story is my way of sharing that you are not alone. I see you. I hear you. And, I honor you.

Thank you for reading and seeing my heart
-writer with an open heart

Chapter 1: A secret

Watching from the living room window, I gazed at a small crowd of people slowly making their way towards my neighbor's home - solemn, heads down and tears falling from their cheeks. The mood was somber.

My parents were amongst the crowd. Dad was quiet and removed - like usual. Mom was consoling others, loving and nurturing - *like usual*, yet her typical happy-go-lucky personality was muted, and her coloring pale.

I don't remember my neighbor's name or even recall her age. I can't even visualize her face. I just remember that she was young - too young, too beautiful and too good to die. Another victim of cancer. One of many I would come to know.

Neighbors, friends and family mourned and turned their heads towards the sky almost to ask why God would take someone so young - it just wasn't fair. My neighbor's death ignited the ultimate question, *"will I be next?"*

I watched the parade of sad friends and neighbors from behind a protective glass across the street. With a single tear making its way down my tiny eight-year old face, I thought, "she knows my secret."

A secret that I kept from my friends and teachers. A secret I would feverishly write on napkins or scribble on any loose-leaf paper I could find. A secret that when I felt brave enough to share, I would whisper into my coveted stuffed animals' ears.

Besides a life-sized Big Bird stuffed animal, this was a secret I never told anyone. Not even my best friend, my mom.

The neighbor across the street, *the woman too young, too beautiful and too good to die*, now knows my secret, I stubbornly thought. She now knows I allowed him to touch me. She knows I didn't stop the game, which he insisted we played whenever mom and dad were not home.

"Walk on my back," he would ask earnestly then demand to be obeyed as I desperately tried to find an excuse to leave.

He would remove his shirt, lay face down on the carpet in his room and motion for me to walk on his back. The catch? Each time I lost my balance, I had to remove an article of clothing. It was the game. And the rule.

This would happen until my scrawny eight-year old body was completely exposed as I stood in his room naked. And, then he would explore. Every inch of me wanted to move, scream and run. But I didn't - I never did. And, I never told.

And as I sat perched like a cat in the window watching the memorial across the street, I realized that I was exposed yet again.

The neighbor knows I was abused by the hands of my older brother, and I allowed him to touch me, forcing me to do things I didn't want to do nor understand and convincing me that it was my fault.

After all, I didn't do anything to stop it.

Chapter 2: A phone call *(present day)*

It's was a cold winter night as we drove through the Sierra Mountains, slowly navigating the snow-filled roads making our way to the familiar yet complete unknown.

I was watching Google maps intently on my phone, instructing my husband as turns approached and nervously focusing my energy on anything but the barrage of 'what ifs' running through my head.

Jack, my husband was maintaining his calm while driving some of the most dangerous streets in the dead of winter.

We were about to embark on a very bad, very depressing and very difficult week - the kind of week that lasts a lifetime and changes everything you know in an instance. A week we had no idea at the time we would face. Yet could sense it was around the bend.

Earlier that day, I received a call from my ex-sister-in-law, Mindy who begrudgingly shared the latest Craig drama. "Your brother had a stroke or seizure. I'm not sure. I'm just sharing what I was told."

Words I thought and said aloud still haunt me today. "I don't care, Mindy. I really don't."

No, I'm not callus. I'm just over it.

I've been through my brother *having* a brain tumor, kidney failure, glaucoma, heart disease, cancer - in every facet and crevice of his body no less. Craig had a flare for the dramatics. And I fell victim one too many times.

I did my due diligence, almost perfunctorily, calling the hospital to verify Craig's newest illness. But this time was different. The nurse on the other line didn't say "no, sorry ma'am, but there's no patient by that name."

This time was real. This time the phone call was *that* phone call.

A nurse, ignoring all HIPAA laws and hospital protocol, shared that my brother was unconscious and in very serious condition.

"Oh honey, you can't talk to your brother. You need to get here right away. There's not much time."

Thanks to that nameless nurse, I made the decision to get my family en route - calling my dad to share that this time was real and eventually yelling at him to please take me seriously.

I made arrangements with work and packed the vehicle for God knows what. What do you pack to visit a sibling in the CCU? How do you prepare? Guess what, you don't.

As we survived our first snow storm in the better part of a decade, we traveled down the hill into Reno - the biggest little city. My old stomping grounds.

A place I haven't seen since getting into a physical fight with my brother and taking a $100 taxi from the capital to the airport - in snow.

Damn, Craig, always making me travel through inclement weather. One of our many arguments we would have and one that seemed poetic as I drove past familiar landmarks - memories of childhood and college racing through my head. Thoughts of Craig. Questions of what we were walking into. Fear of the unknown. Or rather, fear recognizing that this time could be it.

After we made our way to the hotel to check-in, we traveled the longest four-minute drive to the hospital. It was cold, yet I was emotionless, immune to the freezing temperatures.

We wandered through buildings, attempting to find our way without asking too many questions. I, for one, didn't want to make eye contact. It was as if everyone knew what I was about to see, and I didn't want to meet their gaze to avoid reality as long as possible.

As we took the elevator to the fifth floor, turned the corner and walked through the double doors, my heart stopped. I somehow willed myself to pick up the phone outside of the barricade of the CCU and managed to articulate my name, relation and patient's name.

"Hello, this is Casey Gary Caleb," using my full name to appear more mature, able to handle what I was about to walk into. "I'm patient, Craig Gary's sister."

Silence was met on the receiving end until a nurse sighed and pushed the button to open the door. "Beep." My silence was finally broken.

We received clearance and walked the long corridor to Craig's room. My breath was abruptly taken from me as I turned the corner to see my brother, at 40-years old, strapped from every end with needles, pumps, IVs and machines - almost decorating his body.

A nurse rambled a bunch of nonsense to me as I approached his face, noting a small twitch of his foot when I called his name. "Craig...(gulp) it's me. Your little sister. I'm here. You finally got me here." I said half-jokingly to remove the tension from my own soul.

After pretending to absorb the lowdown of his status, I stood awkwardly at his bedside, overtly aware of my husband's eyes on me, concerned that I might just melt. My stubbornness wouldn't allow my body to fall but I knew the truth. My heart dropped to my feet with the same sinking feeling I had when I learned my mom had terminal cancer and had two-months to live.

Chapter 3: A Christmas morning

Christmas morning, 1989. A faint sound of familiar music played in the distance, as my eight-year-old body flew out of bed with excitement.

Christmas was magical in our household - mixed with German traditions, yummy food and love. Dad didn't drink as much. While he was still solemn and removed, he was at least not angry or drunk or both. I took the positive wherever and whenever I could.

Craig still seemed like a kid, excited for all that came with this time of year.

And mom was buzzing about with preparations for the perfect Christmas in her festive pajamas and huge smile permanently plastered, showing off her dimples and crooked teeth. She was a beautiful woman who was painfully self-conscious and overly kind - just never kind to herself. Another lesson I pocketed and stubbornly harbored for years.

Walking the hallway that Christmas morning, memories of dad and Craig's altercation when Craig snuck out his bedroom window with the ladder from his bunk bed - blood, broken glass, screams – were a distant memory.

Instead, my heart and mind were replaced with sounds of mom's favorite holiday songs from her time in Germany, the most delicious, soft sugar cookies and the smell of coffee, German potatoes, eggs and pancakes.

Christmas tingled every sense in the best kind of way. It was never about the presents, for me. It was about this refreshing, festive air that made everything seem like it was going to be okay.

The tree, surrounded with color coordinated wrapped gifts spilling out to the fireplace, was decorated with colored lights and tinsel.

We adorned the tree just a few weeks earlier with handmade ornaments that my mom insisted she loved but strategically placed as a filler in the back of the tree, a delicate angel passed down from generations to generations, and the most eclectic collection of trimmings from mom's childhood and incessant Hallmark shopping.

Not included, anything from my dad's childhood. His family's only tradition was passing my dad from relative to relative, instilling the notion that he was never wanted. And never loved.

Perhaps that's why he prefers to be alone. Relationships and family only disappointed him.

Before opening gifts, mom had a tradition to ensure both parents had coffee in hand, we each enjoyed one of her delicious sugar cookies and took in the smell and sounds of Christmas morning.

It wasn't about the presents - it was about the time together. One of which was happy, rid of alcoholic induced arguments and safe of Craig's hand. It felt free. It was as if Christmas was a protective zone - no issues in the Gary family. All was well.

With snow outside of our Tahoe home, the prospect of sledding in our midst, we opened our gifts, one by one, dad filming the festivities with his oversized VHS camcorder resting uncomfortably on his shoulder.

I remember feeling guilty - why was I lucky to receive all these gifts? A Maxi Barbie, a completely renovated dollhouse, several delicate doilies.

My head envisioned those who did not have a Christmas morning. And my heart would hurt.

This year I wanted to contribute where I could. So, I searched through my toys and carefully wrapped brand new McDonald's figurines, excitedly placing in cocoons of Kleenex hinged together with Scotch tape that I carefully tucked inside Craig and my parents' stockings.

It was my turn to give back - participate in Christmas and the art of gifting. Little did I know the act of giving was an innate calling I wouldn't answer for many years to come.

Chapter 4: A father/son relationship *(present day)*

Dad finally arrived to witness the latest mess Craig got himself into - maybe the final mess, we don't know. Truly, it didn't matter. This was fucked up to say the least.

I picked up dad from the airport and he appeared so small, fragile and old. This was too much for him, I thought. He cannot endure another loss.

Immediately I felt protective and wanted to avoid the issue at hand, continue driving past the hospital, past the hotel and out of Reno. I just wanted to free my dad of the pain I knew he would face once he set foot into Craig's room.

But as I drove him to the hospital, I realized this was a rite of passage. A father whose relationship with his son has been forever in perils had to say his goodbyes, if that's what it came to. This was a necessary evil, as much as it pained me to realize and for my dad to do.

The CCU seemed like a new space in the day, rays of sunshine filled the halls and rooms - almost creating a pleasant atmosphere. Yet, as we made the walk of shame, as it came to be known in my head, reality set in.

seventeen

My dad made little noise or movement as he approached Craig, lifeless in the bed with the faint sound of breathalyzers and respirators continuously making their presence known. He just had a single tear slowly make its way down his face - this was almost more painful to watch than the side glance of my brother's body forcibly moving up and down. So much to be said between the two men. Their relationship in purgatory for more years than I could count. So much pain. Now, little time to heal. It was life's sweet injustice rearing its ugly head.

Chapter 5: A note

It's 1991. Craig's senior year of high school. He only attended a couple of weeks and never graduated. A smart mind wasted. Damn.

As my parents and I drove along the Oregon trail and listened to music from *American Tail* - with Fievel singing about his own separation, life and love - I remember looking out the window at the roaming cattle wondering where my brother was at that moment. Scared, overwhelmed and a bit impressed by the gumption he had to run away with his high school love, Abby.

Months, days, hours have flown by with no word or indication of where he could be - for all we knew, he could be dead.

My parents were distant during this time in our lives - not sure what emotions to show their 10-year old daughter, not realizing I absorbed their behavior and picked up on the urgency to locate Craig. We felt like time was running out.

Dad stopped drinking alcohol as though that was going to bring Craig home. Instead he turned to O'Doul's to still taste his vice while painfully trying to replace the pain he felt for his only son's disappointment, betrayal and dismissal.

Mom immersed herself in church, attending religiously as if to make up for our family misdoings.

Driving through Oregon on a hunch Craig and Abby may be in the area was surreal. I remember feeling like I was in a movie.

Just days earlier, a private investigator - hired by Abby's parents - knocked on our door, accusing us of holding Abby hostage. Turned out my rendition of a gymnastics routine on the stairs and the window leading to the outside convinced the PI it was Abby. I suppose we had similar features, both with olive-toned skinned, brown hair and presumably innocent.

The anonymous tip to Pendleton, Oregon was fruitless. We located Craig and Abby's beat-up clunker, but there was no trace of the love-struck teens. The search continued.

I could feel the breath escape my parent's chest - and somehow, I felt responsible. I should have reported the note I found in Craig's room, listing the menu of survival items.

Things to take:
    -Toilet paper
    -Pot, pan, dish, silverware
    -Flash light
    -Jumper cables

-Tool box
-Blanket, pillow, towel
-Snow boots
-Leather jacket
-Winter clothes
-Cash

But I didn't share, and I was too late…

Chapter 6: A social worker *(present day)*

The nurses report little improvement - concern about the long-term effects. He may have gone too far this time.

Dad, Jack and I sat in a clinically white room, pacing - nervously holding on to the side of the bed, occasionally touching Craig's arm and hand to remind ourselves of the reality. But it never felt real.

Doctor reports in - routinely, almost aggressively - to provide the latest: multiple seizures, little reaction, thick blood, non-responsive. Tests regarding his brain stimulation were mentioned and EKGS were discussed. It was all a blur.

All I could think about were memories of Craig's laugh, thinking about the last time we saw each other months prior in Twin Lakes. Sitting around the campfire, drinking beer and Captain and cokes, remembering mom like we always did.

Despite everything, we were a family - full of love, life and memories. Regardless of the fights, unresolved arguments and pain, we loved one another.

Doctors, nurses, PAs and assistants shuffled in and out - all with the same mannerisms and demeanor, wondering what could have happened to lead to this life-altering moment. Debating what kind of family, we are.

Or what kind of family we were. Shit.

As we left the CCU, a social worker approached our family - cataloging details of the family, capturing details of the sad truth our family had to face. Notes of divorced family, unstable household, drugs and lack of insurance were jotted down. My dad shamefully lowered his head.

We left to make the four-mile trek back to the hotel to reconvene and try to savor food, pretend life will go on and that things will be okay.

We all knew the truth: the Gary's will face another loss. Another dramatic event...what's new. People can't even feel badly for us anymore. They just feel sorry for us and keep their distance.

Chapter 7: A beater

Christmas eve, 1991. The same German music played in the distance, the smell of Spinach Squares permeated the home, pastry puffs and sugar cookies were stubbornly present, but the house felt empty.

Craig and Abby have been missing since September with no word. It was truly fucked up. My parents were devastated. And, I was pissed.

To couple the faux merriment and awaken the home, the phone rang.

It was Craig calling for mom. Soft spoken, timid and nostalgic, Craig called to tell mom he found himself taken in by a random family, baking cookies. And once the kind, unknowingly innocent woman asked Craig to lick the beaters, Craig burst into tears and asked to call home.

Food was a large part of our family. My mom's cooking, while I'm sure I reflect nostalgically and perhaps idealistically, was the best food I've ever had. From her mouthwatering sugar cookies, to her party-must Spinach Squares, my mom made food with love. And you could taste it with every bite.

Most memories were associated with the taste of the holidays or whatever celebration or benign

Sunday evening my mom cooked for our family. And Craig, a big lover of all foods, was mom's most dedicated taster and beater licker.

Months following the phone call that perked mom's spirits with the relief that her son was alive, Craig finally opened up as to where he stayed with the old woman who asked him to lick the beater.

And, the family traveled to Kettle Falls, Washington to pick-up Craig, Abby and their yappy dog.

And unborn child.

Chapter 8: A purposeful response *(present day)*

The thing about Craig is his resiliency. *Or was.*

Craig never gave up. He didn't even give up on his marriages with two women who gave everything they had to love him. They just didn't realize that he didn't love anybody but himself. It wasn't a personality flaw. It was an epidemic.

Abby wanted the divorce. Her relationship with Craig was toxic, to say the least. There was a history of fights to which neighbors called the cops in hopes of protecting one-year old, William and silencing the incessant arguments that penetrated their shared walls.

William was the victim in the marriage, just an innocent bystander often left to eat Cheetos for dinner while seated in a soiled diaper. It was dysfunction at its best. And just heartbreaking to watch unfold.

Craig's second wife, Mindy left after she learned of an affair. An affair that not only compromised their marriage and family but also their bank account.

Sure, Mindy stayed despite the threesome she begrudgingly facilitated with Craig's "secret" not so secret crush. She stayed when he raised his hand to her face and punched a hole in the wall instead – almost like a fair warning of what's to come. She even stayed when Craig was accused of messing around with a 17-year old girl and the cops broke into their home to take his computer as evidence of statutory rape.

But this indiscretion was different or the straw that broke the camel's back. This time Craig racked up a $400 plus hotel stay during a time that he couldn't pay bills and the electricity was intermittently on.

With this final straw, Mindy found a lawyer, filed a divorce, requested full custody of the kids and left.

The size of her home and the fear of not knowing where her kids' next meal would come from didn't stop Mindy from leaving my brother. I will always respect her for that. She left. I'm still learning how.

In response to Mindy finally exposing her ovaries and leaving an abusive and cheating husband, Craig was furious – excusing any of his behavior as reasoning for the separation.

"How could she break-up the family?" Craig would question, hastily.

He never took responsibility for the demise in their relationship. Heck, he never took responsibility for anything.

He was clueless that his actions had consequences. A true narcissist met with borderline personality disorder, Craig was the center of everyone's world and was never wrong, in his eyes. If you disagreed, shit would get ugly.

Craig had spirit, whether good, bad or incredibly inappropriate. And in this moment, strapped from every facet of his body, Craig's spirit responded and reacted, riding the hospital bed sideways - attempting to rip out his IVs and wires.

This reaction provided us hope. Despite the damage, he is in there. I couldn't help but be proud, despite the fucked-up shit Craig did to me and those who loved him most. He was a fighter – we all are.

And, there's still much to live for…

Chapter 9: A backyard wedding

In the backyard of Abby's parents, manufactured wedding decor was strategically placed about in effort to create a celebration for Craig and Abby. But everyone from parents, siblings and *heck,* the next-door neighbor knew the truth. Disappointment could be felt, and disapproval was noticed by more than just me.

I remember thinking that Craig and Abby looked so sad on what was supposed to be the happiest day of their lives. It made weddings and relationships confusing to me.

A small gathering of supportive friends and family sat in white, fold-up plastic chairs. Light music from a boombox played Mozart as a pregnant Abby walked down the makeshift aisle, outlined with purple plastic flowers.

Abby's pregnant belly, which almost mocked her laced white dress and strategically placed baby's breath about her hair, was the focal point. Everyone's eyes inadvertently went straight to Abby's belly as she sheepishly smiled, revealing her braces and overgrown gums from months of neglect.

Abby did not have medical care while she and Craig lived in Kettle Falls– a small town just before the Canadian border.

They settled in this picturesque town because they were scared they would be caught crossing into Canada, their initial destination.

Resembling 90's television star Alyssa Milano, Abby was often stopped with the inquisitive and almost accusatory question, "I know you, right?"

This attention concerned Craig and Abby, and they were convinced their photo was plastered on milk cartons, circulated across the country. So, they decided to find refuge in an unassuming town with less than 1500 people.

Like the town they escaped to, their wedding ceremony was understated. Almost sweet in a way.

Craig's face was one of a person in love...a little uncertain but still with hope and promise.

I think that's what pains me the most. Craig had dreams - some realized. Some swept under. Some never came to fruition.

The wedding was festive and lively. Homemade desserts and appetizers were enjoyed. Beer and tequila were consumed. And the lives of Abby, Craig and an unborn William were forcibly celebrated despite the aching feeling that things would not work out as planned.

Chapter 10: A sense of hope *(present day)*

Next day at the hospital, we entered the halls with a renewed sense of hope. The air seemed to be lighter. And even the sight of Craig and his barrage of needles, cords and breathing tubes seemed less intimidating.

As always, there was a silver of promise. Much like the number of times that Craig would change his ways.

He would start telling the truth, or his version of the truth, stop cheating on his partners and live a life of integrity.

He would be on track - for a few months, sometimes for a year or so. Then, things would unravel, and Craig would use his creative storytelling and sneaky ways to cover his transgressions

It was a cycle. And a renewed sense of hope would be squandered with the reminder that the "Craig's" of the world do not change.

Just as I felt disappointment the countless times before, our hope was diminished when met with our reality.

Craig's earlier moment of riding the hospital bed sideways was combatted with the results from his EKGs. He has inoperable brain damage. There isn't much the doctors can do…or that we can fix.

Chapter 11: A boy with skies

In the delivery room, the Gary family felt renewed – it was the dawn of a new life and thus, a new beginning.

William, Craig's first born, was brought into this world "...with skis," the doctor announced excitedly.

Craig was very proud of his son and the potential of this new person, life and love. Despite being a kid himself, William represented a new chapter and a clean slate.

Sitting in my parent's living room, the blinds were drawn yet the sunny September rays filtered in. William was snuggled in his bassinet.

I, now an aunt, had such a strong fascination for this tiny human with oversized feet. I just wanted to hold him. Let him know that no matter what, I cared. Immediately I felt a kinetic bond - little did I know that William and I would be forever linked by love and loss.

My mom, appearing older and heavier, perfunctorily grabbed the video camera – as we always do - to capture these moments as if to convince herself she was supportive of the situation.

The once vivacious woman who was the center of our universe was now quiet and removed.

Mom didn't have a lot to say during this time. She would smile and laugh, but her eyes looked vacant and distance.

She insisted, however, that things would improve. Craig and Abby would make it. Everything would be okay.

I've taken a page from mom's book of blind positivity and applied to my own life. It's blindly misleading.

But through mom's forced smile, her on command laughs and pension for hiding behind the camera, we all knew the truth. Just no one said or admitted it out loud.

Chapter 12: A time to call William *(present day)*

The doctor came in with the results.

His once chipper voice was masked with disappointment. Fear, almost. "Coward," I thought. And then immediately regretted.

The brain damage was too significant for any kind of hope that Craig would recover. His chances were slim to none. The only game plan was to wait. Days, weeks, months, years. He could survive but for what? A life of eating from a tube?

I took a forced swallow, fighting back tears to salvage my father's emotion.

It was time to call William.

Chapter 13: A trip to Apple Hill

The family, in an effort to be or at least appear to be united, traveled to Apple Hill in Placerville, California.

Like many families in Northern Nevada, this quintessential farm became a fall tradition - eating apple pie, petting farm animals, making crafts and selecting pumpkins kicked off the holiday season.

This year was a bit different, however. It seemed less festive, perhaps, and more obligatory bringing Craig, Abby and one-year old William in tow.

After William was born, Craig and Abby played the part of doting parents and happy couple. But they were still kids themselves: Craig was 19 and Abby just turned 17. They were too young for this kind of responsibility. The odds were against them and things started to change. Quickly.

Dad, continuously removed and solemn, routinely did his job and captured the memories with our trusty oversized VHS, resting on his shoulder.

Poor dad, that damn, ridiculously heavy camera was strapped to his shoulder like a commitment he couldn't shake.

He's since had shoulder surgery due to overuse. Wonder if there's any connection. Family is really a pain, literally and figuratively.

Mom, continued to be less positive and not herself - but as if her emotions never mattered, she shoved her feelings deep inside and only showcased a forced smile and laugh.

It was her coping mechanism. And stubbornness to maintain the family, no matter what. Sometimes I wonder if the pension to keep us together was more for appearance. "What will the neighbor's think?"

We ordered our customary apple pies and ate them at the picnic tables, strategically placed by the adorable rust colored windmill and creek. The sounds of fall were amongst us, but the spirit couldn't penetrate the dark cloud that seemed to hover the Gary family.

Craig, who obviously gained weight from the stress and lack of a healthy diet, looked extremely exhausted and removed. He ate his pie and didn't say much, avoiding any eye contact with his family.

Abby was painfully unaware of her role as a mother and often had to be reminded that William was in her care. She ate her pie and didn't even look up at her son who was being fed a little apple filling by my mom.

William didn't make eye contact either. His gaze was lovingly focused on his grandma – the one constant in his chaotic life. The bond these two shared was one of necessity for William and guilt from my mom. Regardless, the love was palpable.

Abby would go on about her day, clumsily holding William as if she was a four-year old girl halfheartedly carrying her ragged floppy-eared stuffed animal.

"Abby, Abby, ABBY!" We each found ourselves yelling out of frustration, trying to ensure she didn't drop William. Let alone protect him from the sun, other people's flailing arms or roaming livestock.

Even in her arms, William wasn't a part of her. There was zero connection and their relationship was vapid.

To this day, I firmly believe William's inability to maintain a relationship and his pension for pathological lying is a direct result of his biological parents. Despite the fact that he spent less than three years with them combined, he absorbed some of their more unattractive qualities. And was a product of their selfish parenting style.

Watching Abby precariously walk down the dirt path in Apple Hill towards the turkeys with the smell of fall in the air, was entertaining. Her walk was akin to a baby giraffe in its first few minutes of life, trying to navigate a slight downgrade with a mixture of small pebbles and palm sized rocks. It was comical until you realized she was in her own world, raising a kid while being one.

She never turned around to look at William nor was concerned about Craig carrying the diaper bag over his shoulder and stroller in his arms. William – and Craig, for that matter, were the last things on her mind.

As the relationship digressed, Craig played both mom and dad while he also had the mentality of a teenager. William didn't have a chance.

Chapter 14: A Red Cross moment *(present day)*

Not knowing what to do next, I paced Craig's room. Going through his plastic bag of items, searching the internet for advice and religiously checking Facebook for updates on Craig's page.

While my body felt scattered, my mind kept pulling to the Red Cross – a place I served as an AmeriCorps member in Alaska and found myself back in action in San Diego, responding to the historic 2007 wildfires.

Red Cross was home to me, in a way - and serves as a conduit for military personnel facing life threatening situations, marking it easier for families to connect during difficult times.

I didn't want to mix my personal and professional worlds, but before I knew it, I found myself calling the Red Cross to issue a request to send William to Reno. At the time, he was in the US Army, living on base in Kentucky.

As I navigated a website I was intimately aware of, it dawned on me the severity of this call. This was sealing Craig's fate. He isn't going to make it, is he? Fuck.

The phone clicked, and a familiar voice was on the other line.

"Casey? Is that you? Casey who used to work for the Red Cross?

"...yes, it's me...," I replied hesitantly.

As fate would have it, while I called the national Red Cross line, a friendly, familiar voice from San Diego picked up.

It was a reminder that no matter what, I would be okay.

Chapter 15: A doorbell ring

After several arguments, terrifying fights, dramatic episodes, Craig and Abby finally parted ways.

The neighbors were relieved. My parents were concerned. William's future became a little less certain.

Abby had custody of William but was nowhere to be found. Rumors of drugs, promiscuous sex and even prostitution were circling but we had no clue where she was living.

Craig moved in with Johnny - a long-time friend from Carson. They lived in Reno and worked at a local grocery store. Far from any responsibility of parenthood.

Craig was living a college lifestyle without having to take a class or pay for a book. His absolute dream. Or at least that's what he made you believe – he was always very convincing.

One morning my grandma, a strong-headed, hardworking German woman whose visits were at minimum a month long, was in the kitchen reminiscing about who knows.

Her accent was so strong, making comprehension require a dual language in both English and German. I made out about 50% of the words she spoke to me.

The house was bright and cheery. We were all happy go lucky, enjoying liverwurst and butter sandwiches on German bread.

The day felt light. To this day, if a day seems too good to be true, I fear an unexpected twist. I'm always prepared.

Ding -dong. Ding -dong.

"Mom, I'll get it!!" I yelled as I scurried from the family room in a matching tracksuit with my permed hair pulled into a bright pink scrunchie. It was the 90s look at its best.

I opened the door to a scene I'll never forgot. It's seared into my memory and the very fibers of my being.

There I was, staring at my two-year old nephew, William in a car seat. Alone, barely clothed, with a note from Abby. No diaper bag.

"Please take him," it read in scurried handwriting on the back of a Longs Drugs receipt – cigarettes where the only item purchased. My heart sank.

"MOM….," I squealed, my high pitch voice scaring the cats. My mom came running over as I slowly started to feel my hands, feet and body again.

Just like that, life changed.

Chapter 16: A night of laughs *(present day)*

Death is a funny thing. No, I'm serious - death can be
funny. And I've always found myself dead center
(pun unintended) between crying myself to sleep to
laughing so hard my stomach hurt.

I truly believe life is about the duality – the idea that
you can be both happy and sad, at the same time.
It's recognition that life is constantly changing.

I learned this at a very young age. It's like my secret
power, knowing that death is a part of life and one
of life's only guarantees. That, and everything is here
to teach you something.

After the hospital, we needed a drink. Or a few.

After hitting up the nearest liquor store, my dad,
Jack and I walked through the lobby with drinks in
tow, a plastic bag and my mom's urn in hand.

My mom's urn is not modest – it's large with four
chiseled columns, a large brass prayers hand and an
inscription which reads, "My hero and my teacher."

A lyric from song depicting a late father from a local
band who I lamented on, cried over and mourned
with – a song I played in my head for years.

Unfortunately, the band's namesake was *Uncut,* craftly appointed as all the members have an uncircumcised penis.

Death can be humorous.

And, as we walked through crowds of people and the front desk staff gazed on with curiosity, I couldn't help but laugh.

The prospect of seeing a disheveled, depressed-looking family with a liquor bottle, beer cans, chips and wine peeking out of a plastic bag, and an older man carrying a cumbersome urn was just too much for me. It was pure comedy - like a scene out of an episode of *Arrested Development*.

Most people staying at the hotel casino were visiting Reno to gamble, drink and have a good time.

We, in contrast, were sharing in their space of cigarettes, prospect and hope, drowning in our own grief.

I don't know but the juxtaposition made me laugh so hard that Jack and my dad couldn't help but join in. Now we looked deranged with our vices and mom's ashes in hand losing our shit in the middle of the lobby - this made us laugh even more.

Chapter 17: A choke-hold

I know what it's like to live between violence and peace. And, by virtue I embody both, marking it difficult sometimes to know what is right from wrong.

My life has always been blurred between black and white. You can say that I live in gray. So, did Craig.

After William was "delivered" to my parents' front door, Craig decided to continue living with his buddy, Johnny in Reno. Selfish asshole.

There were rumors that Abby continued to visit Craig despite the fact that she moved on with a new boyfriend. And, supposedly sold herself to make money.

My father, fed up with the back and forth lies, decided to surprise Craig with a visit. I tagged along.

Serendipitously, so did Abby's new boyfriend and his batch of misfit friends. Craig, for the second time I'm aware of, was about to be jumped.

The first was in our front driveway. I was nine. Craig was 16. My innocent cries and pleas stopped the two boys from punching and kicking Craig as they fled.

Craig, while mildly injured, got off from the ground - bloodied lip, ruffled hair, sweat and bruises – took one look at me and left.

This time, the match was met with an army of people - unknowingly aware of one another. Except me.

As soon as Abby's boyfriend approached Craig, with Johnny on his left and my dad off to the side, I stepped in front, stretched my right arm out and wrapped my tiny 13-year old hand around this man's neck.

Again, I diffused the situation. Craig took one look at me, turned around and went inside his condo.

I didn't see him again for several years, when he returned from Mississippi for a visit.

Chapter 18: An adoption

After weeks of putting the puzzle back together, my mom and dad sought help from a life-long friend, Noah Wilson.

Noah was the son of the wealthy family that hired my mom twice a week to clean their three-story, million-dollar home overlooking the pristine Lake Tahoe waters.

We met the Wilson's in Canandaigua, New York – my birthplace. My mom cleaned their home every Monday and Friday and made a good chunk of change under the table.

But she was more than just their dishwasher, duster, bed-maker and trash remover. My mom became a part of the Wilson's family.

And once I was born, I went with my mom every day to clean houses. In fact, I cleaned with my mother from the time I was old enough to dust the bookshelves until two months before she passed away. It was our bonding time. And as a result, I'm highly organized and OCD. But my house is immaculate. Always.

Craig had run off to Biloxi, Mississippi with his trusty friend Johnny. He wanted to continue to flex his "college years" muscles and have fun in the south, ignoring all responsibility.

Abby was nowhere to be found. But we didn't give a shit. She had become dead to us.

So, it was the four of us, navigating a new chapter in our lives. It was time to provide William with a permanent, stable home.

Noah, a successful lawyer in Reno, knew our family.

He knew that Craig ran away, impregnated his 17-year old girlfriend and was involved in a tumultuous two-year relationship. He knew every skeleton in our proverbial closet and loved us anyway. Accepted the Gary's for who we were and didn't judge.

Instead, he offered his expertise, time and professional services to us to help propel us forward.

Noah has always served as a beacon of hope for me and my family. For that, I'm forever grateful. I fear that I could never repay the favor but then again, sometimes people just do things out of the goodness of their heart. And, that was Noah.

I don't recall the details of the conversation my parents had with Noah – discussing the situation and their hopes to adopt William. But I remember the feeling, that of moving from impermanence to finality.

As a 13-year old teen, I knew our lives would change once again.

I also knew that my feelings were not on the table for discussion. I needed to rise to the occasion and become a big sister. I needed to follow the rules and not ruffle feathers. I needed to be a good kid and not cause my parents anymore trouble. I was worried they couldn't take much more – for their health and their marriage.

I recognized that I needed to take a back seat as my parents and William needed me more than I needed them.

And, that's the dynamic that has continued...

Chapter 19: A break-in *(present day)*

You know the old saying that when it rains, it pours. It happens every time.

Just when you think the universe dealt you the only shitty hand you could possibly imagine, you are served another and another and another. And guess what? You just deal.

Sitting in the hospital for what felt like years but in reality, was only a couple of days, there wasn't much improvement.

The nurses and doctors came and went, Craig's friends tried to schedule visits in the CCU and friends or family on Facebook asked questions about Craig's whereabouts.

"Was it the cancer?

"Oh, poor Craig - he was looking awfully skinny."

This was difficult to facilitate because I never knew what "truth" Craig told whom - what did these "friends" know about Craig? Why are they bringing up cancer? Didn't they know he was a drug addict and serial cheater?

Craig's charisma was palpable. He could convince anyone of anything. And, they wouldn't question a thing. That's the power Craig had. He was a charmer. Always has been.

But when he didn't get his way, he would turn on you faster than you could blink your eye. A narcissist through and through.

As soon as his actions, words or character were questioned, he attacked as if he had nothing to lose. And as I learned, he didn't.

Sitting in Craig's room, I got a call from Mindy. Someone broke into Craig's house and cut the electrical wires. This was perplexing - why would someone do this? Who would do this?

We decided to drive to Carson to investigate yet we recognized the risk we were taking by entering Craig's house. Would my dad and I become liable for whatever shit Craig got himself into?

We arrived at Craig's house around dusk. The house, which once had an air of hope, love and happiness - felt stale.

It smelled of bachelor and was uncharacteristically dirty for Craig, who - like me - has always been OCD.

His fridge was empty. And the place appeared to be turned over: furniture out of place, things knocked over.

I made my way upstairs into Craig's office, which was the only place in the house that was clean. It was spotless, in fact - neat piles of mail stacked evenly on the desk.

Craig owned a cleaning business. At one point, he was the biggest cleaning company in Carson, scoring the largest hospital as a client - the very place Craig was taken after the stroke.

Feeling desperate for answers, I started to open the envelopes: past due notices for taxes, mortgage and vehicle payments. Dozens of them. It was overwhelming to me and in doing the math in my head, I calculated Craig was about $50,000 behind in his mortgage and over $70,000 behind in taxes.

I started to realize Craig's demise. And, I started to understand Craig.

There was even a letter indicating Craig was being sued by a former employee - something about an illegal hire. I couldn't make sense of everything other than to know that Craig was utterly fucked.

No wonder communication was lacking. No wonder he lost so much weight. No wonder his house appeared disheveled.

Craig had backed himself into a corner that would be difficult for anyone to escape.

I started to cry, knowing Craig was better off dead.

Chapter 20: A church comedy

My family and I shopped churches like sweaters, trying each one on for size until we found the right fit. Poor William was just along for the ride.

As a new family and Craig off in Mississippi with little to no contact, my mom forced us to look to religion as a savior from our messy past and indiscretions.

We tried out almost every church in Carson – excuse any Mormon or Jehovah Witness places of worship for obvious reasons.

There was the tiny 50-person steeple church with modest funding, and where I was forced to play a solo flute performance for the Christmas play just two-weeks after learning how to play. Thanks, mom.

Then the Episcopalian church where members of the congregation randomly yelled in tongues, startling William and me with each bellowed cry, hand raised to the sky and hum in unison. Again, thanks, mom.

One particular church visit had my father and me laughing uncontrollably and my mother - well, crossed-armed with her lips stubbornly pursed in complete embarrassment.

On our one and only visit to this church, William was pulled to the front of the pulpit along with every other 3-5-year-old in the congregation before my parents could say no. Not realizing that he never rehearsed let alone knew what they were about to sing, they placed William front and center.

As the only kid who didn't know the words, William cried uncontrollably with his adorable, quarter-sized glasses with a blue truck eye-patch over his left eye fogging up with his tears.

The juxtaposition of the happily singing kids next to William, mixed with the scenario of our lives, was just too much for my father and I to handle.

Sometimes you just have to laugh. So, we did, making a scene and pissing my mother off even more.

Poor William. We never went back to that church.

Chapter 21: Just another day *(present day)*

After sneaking around Craig's home and exposing Craig's current lifestyle – drugs, parties, underage girls - it was time to come to terms.

What options do we have? What options does Craig have?

If he makes it through, what's going to happen…

It was one of the lowest moments in my life. And for my dad - this was devastating. His son was already gone.

Just another day in the hospital.

Chapter 22: A visit

After several years, Craig came back for a visit. And despite everything, I was excited to see him and share my latest updates.

I was 16, in high school, a part of the student government and on the track, cross-country and ski team. I was growing up, but I was widely immature and oddly innocent for my age. Despite everything.

Craig looked the same except he seemed older and less confidant, losing a bit of his charisma.

He almost resembled a dog who ran away from home, got into scuffles, left hungry and had to overcome a lot to find his way back home. The time scarred him.

Craig also adopted a southern accent and to the day Craig died, he maintained a southern charm.

Adding to the list of life changes, Craig had another child. One that we did not learn of until years later.

It wasn't until Craig was in the hospital did we become aware of the influence Craig had on this child's life. And the woman he had an affair with - a pastor's wife.

In digging through family photos, we stumbled on professional pictures with Craig, the pastor's wife and their son, Sam, that my dad and I realized they were a family.

Sam, who is in his twenties by now, was born with Down Syndrome. That's all we know. And as far as we know, Craig didn't keep contact.

While Craig was in town, he paid little to no attention to William who we clunkily referred to as his little brother.

Craig was able to compartmentalize like no one's business – out of sight, out of mind and heart.

William was made aware of his adoption early on, but we maintained the new status - Craig was his brother, not his father. And that never changed until the day William saw his father strapped to the hospital bed with IVs and wires. To this, William said: "he never wanted me," as he cried on my shoulder.

On this visit, Craig seemed to only pay attention to me, fascinated by the person I was becoming. He was most intrigued by me playing the flute, and he requested me to perform.

As I did as a kid, I obliged. But this time, the performance was innocent and sweet.

Craig cried with perhaps the realization that he no longer recognized his life.

I cried, too. It was a moment I will always remember, smile and cry.

Chapter 23: A first date

Needless to say, I had issues with boys - in high school and, well let's be honest, now. I was inexperienced, goofy and awkward. Luckily boys never approached me.

In high school, I looked like a tween - not a 16-year old girl, supposedly blossoming into a woman. And, I was a goody-goody; you would never find me at a party. I preferred to be home, with my mom and family. To this day, I'm still a homebody.

Sure, I had crushes. There was Brian, the tan hazel-eyed soccer player who had no idea I was alive. That is until I mistakenly talked about him in band – going on and on about how cute he is, not realizing his brother shared the same class and sat directly behind me. Whoops.

And then there was the Senior Class President and basketball star who was as obtainable as a movie star, in my opinion.

It wasn't until I had a thing for Zack - a 6'4" redhead who apparently had a thing for me too - that I attempted to be social.

We ran cross-country together and flirted here and there. At least I think that him tackling me during capture-the-flag and yelling out in front of the entire team "eew...are you on your period?" constituted as flirting. I knew I wasn't, but his accusation made me question if I miscounted the days. Nope - just ketchup. Jerk.

Along came Sadie Hawkins where the girls invite the boys, and I made it my mission to ask Zack to the dance.

I grew up the courage to ask him on a date, which I know took a lot of ovaries as I don't recount how or what I said. But after I asked him, I ignored and avoided Zack for several weeks. I struggled with the boys.

The time came for the dance, and for dinner, we decided to take my best friends, Amelia and Brenda to Taco Bell as an awkward foursome.

After cheap tacos, we drove to campus where the dance was held and dropped off my friends.

Zack made some excuse that he forgot something at his house and asked if we could go back home first.

My instincts told me no, but I obliged. Always did.

Once we made it to his house in the countryside, I realized the need for Zack to go home - he was hosting a rager, also known as my first party.

While at his party, I walked around with my arms positioned close to my chest, holding my black silky purse and blue sweater so not to misplace.

I was wearing the classic maxi, slip dress - very circa 1996. I looked like I was about to sing in front of my church congregation. Not attend a high school party.

I was offered an array of cocktails and beverages. All of which I responded with, "no thank you, I don't drink."

To that, someone handed me a root beer. After a sip, I realized it was root beer schnapps. Assholes. I sneakily hid my not-so-root beer drink on the book shelf, behind a framed family portrait.

Finally, curfew hit, I asked Zack to take me home.

As we made the trek through the dimly lit cross-country road back to my parent's house, Zack pulled over to the side and started to off-road up dirt mounds.

A little frightened by his detour, I reminded him that I needed to be home. To that, his truck stopped working – or so he claimed.

He made all the right gestures as if to "test" to see what the issue could be. And, then he turned and looked at me.

His gaze I recognized. I can thank Craig for that. It was the look of desperation, uncontrolled hormones and opportunity.

I shakily told him I had to be home as I bent down to take off my wedges with one hand on the door handle in preparation to run. This was the age before cell phones.

With that, Zack realized he wasn't going to get in my panties - my first victory in fending off a perverted guy. And just like that, Zack's truck miraculously started, and I finally made it home after my first non-dance.

My parents suspected foul play as my face was pale and my slip dress had come undone.

To this day, my dad thinks I fooled around with Zach. Little does he know, I had just escaped another 'me too' moment.

I later learned this was Zack's modius operandi.

An acquaintance shared a similar experience and luckily her instincts were just as heightened.

Zack's game plan was 0 for 2. What a fucker.

Chapter 24: Mom dropping me off at college

Most kids are excited for college. The prospect of being independent and away from their parents is music to their ears.

For me, I cried leaving high school - the comforting walls with supportive teachers, structure and familiarity was my safe haven. Despite knowing that life is in a state of impermanence, I hate change.

My mom was the one who moved me into my dorm room. A room I shared with my shy and incredibly sweet friend, Tina.

We lived in Manzanita, the oldest building on campus converted into an all-girl dorm. I would share the dorm life with my three closest friends from middle and high school. It was a perfect combination of home and new.

As my mom and I moved in my chest - much like the one from the late 90's show, *Felicity* - coat hanger, clothes, new comforter and all my carefully selected "collegy" things into my dorm, the reality set in. I'm no longer living at home, and my heart started to ache.

I didn't share my breaking heart and overwhelming fear with my mom – I wanted to be mature and independent.

To celebrate my new independence and room akin to Felicity's dorm (or so I wished), my mom and I had a late lunch at the local German restaurant – the one that we frequented often for German bread and liverwurst.

We enjoyed a lovely meal and an even better conversation.

My mom and I were twin flames, best friends and each other's biggest supporter. She was my best friend. And, I was leaving her for a world she didn't know: college. The idea of it was breaking my heart. Little did I know, it was breaking hers, too.

As she dropped me off at my new home, I stood at the window and watched her walk to her vehicle. Her head was down, and her body language solemn.

When she crossed the street, I caught a glimpse of her crying. We both knew our lives were going to be different.

Chapter 25: A sign of cancer

With me away in college, my mom finally decided to go to the doctor. She had not been since I was born - 19 years earlier.

My mom claimed it was a gift for my dad as he had been begging her to go. Her incessant cough and nausea plagued her for more years than I could count.

I distinctly remember a time in elementary school when I woke up to my mom puking in the kitchen sink. She embarrassingly looked at me and asked if I would stay home from school with her that day. As a kid, I thought it was the best thing ever to play hooky with mom. Little did I know that we were on borrowed time.

With my overwhelming excitement to spend the day with mom eating waffles and watching cartoons, she called the school and claimed *I* was sick. I never knew why she lied that day - she was not a fan of not telling the truth. And she insisted I do better than her in school.

My mom never graduated high school. She married my father at age 17 instead.

She was always embarrassed by her lack of education but explained she married young to help her family. With six kids, her parents struggled to keep food on the table, and my mom figured with her out of the picture there would be more to go around.

Mom always sacrificed.

And, I think she always knew she had cancer.

Chapter 26: It's real

One fall afternoon, I was cooking Totino's in my college room tiny microwave, and I got a call. It was from my parents, letting me know we needed to talk.

"It's real," they said with little emotion - I think in effort to keep me assured that everything was going to be okay. Their uncharacteristic tone told me otherwise.

"Mom has cancer, but it's treatable. She will be fine." That was one of the only lies I'm aware of that my parents told me. In their eyes, to protect my innocence. If they only knew.

That weekend I traveled home to be with my mom.

She seemed distant as I tried to comfort her with Sleepy Time tea and circus cookies, two of our favorites. She wasn't interested.

My mom was a newly 45-year old woman, just diagnosed with stage 3 breast cancer. Her only source of income required her to scrub on her knees and have stamina to clean for nine-hours straight.

She was not only worried about her health but her family's future.

In what seemed like a flash, my mom underwent a mastectomy. She lost her right breast. And in a day was home sitting on our living room couch with a drain below her chest.

She was in an incredible pain, crying openly - for once not caring about anyone else or what anyone thought. She fucking hurt.

Neighbors wanted to visit, but I asked them to just send their best wishes. She couldn't bear to visit with anyone.

It was painful to watch, and it still breaks my heart as I reflect.

Chapter 27: Craig marries again

Craig returned to Carson City with a new reputation, a little extra pounds and an adopted southern accent.

Craig continued his stint in the grocery business, working at Smith's. It was there that Craig met his second wife, Mindy.

Mindy, 27 at the time was a single mother of a sweet, little girl named Sherry.

Craig quickly fell in love with the petite blond from the neighboring town, Dayton.

Soon they got married and pregnant with Mason. Craig again created a new family. But had forgotten about William. Nevertheless, Sam. Or, at least we presume.

Chapter 28: Noah to the rescue again *(present day)*

The longer Craig continued to be in the hospital, the more we started to fear the future.

Questions about Craig's stuff and legal troubles lingered. Would we be responsible? Will Craig's mistakes become our unfair burdens? We cannot afford to assume his debt.

We decided to reach out to an old friend – we called Noah.

Traveling through midtown, noting the new art and budding hip cultural scene, we made our way to Noah's law practice, which operated out of a sweet cottage on a tree-lined street.

It was like no time passed seeing Noah again. We quickly caught up on family happenings and then got right into business.

"What are we liable for," I asked, taking my usual place as the responsible one during family events. "What are our options?"

Noah recommended we video Craig's belongings and only take family heirlooms.

The definition of heirloom appeared to be loose, but we were still nervous to make any moves. And hesitant to start this process – it was as if Craig was already gone. In a way, he's always been.

The next day we decided to head to Craig's house. Again.

Chapter 29: A discovery *(present day)*

Walking through Craig's house in daylight was a different experience. The dirty, grime bachelor lifestyle was more evident. The smell seemed to be more pungent. How could Craig live like this? What about Sherry and Mason?

Torn couches, a disheveled kitchen with massive bongs and half smoked blunts spread about the living room, made up a once picturesque living room that Craig and Mindy were proud of.

The backyard, once groomed, green and vibrant, was covered with frozen dog shit and empty beer bottles.

And the garage served as a memorial with a dried-up coffee spill and Craig's mug laying sideways on the ground. There was even a little bit of blood.

This was the spot, just earlier, Craig's employee stood talking as Craig raised his arm to take a sip of coffee. Instead, he dropped the mug and fell to the ground, convulsing uncontrollably. The garage was haunting.

To this day, I'm reminded of this moment when I reach my arm up to take a sip of coffee.

Jack diligently videotaped every square inch of the house – just like dad with every holiday and travel, often filming more of strange woman than the family.

But unlike the bikini clad woman and any half-way attractive female that happened to intersect our family videos, Jack carefully captured Craig's belongings, ensuring to highlight the family heirlooms we planned to take - photos, Grandpa's banjo, the kid's clothes and toys.

At one point, Mindy and the kids joined, packing up their once loving and lively home. Despite the tragedy, Sherry and Mason appeared unemotional. Perhaps denial phase.

For me, the scene was too much to take.

The family convened and started to compile photos, ripping from the photo albums to save space. Not much was exchanged nor said. The mood was solemn.

In mid pull of a photo from Craig and Mindy's wedding in Vegas, our next-door neighbor knocked at the opened front door.

Mr. Rodgers, a Mormon man with the biggest heart and the most curious personality, saw activity outside Craig's home and wanted to check-in after learning the news.

He stood at the front door awkwardly for what felt like hours. He didn't appear to pick up on any social cue that "now is not the time."

Just as my dad desperately tried to escort Mr. Rodgers outside, I discovered an envelope of memories with Craig and his love affair in Mississippi. There were love notes and photos of Sam, their son.

The photos were professionally taken - the kind from Wal-Mart, with the cheesy blue background and stifled poses.

The relationship and child Craig described as accidental and temporary appeared to be more than just that. It looked to be love and resembled a family. It was a side of Craig we never knew.

This discovery prompted me to need a drink.

Chapter 30: My first faux drink

Because my older brother was a fuck up, and my parent's marriage was always on the brink – namely due to alcohol - I didn't drink in high school. And I was rarely in positions to feel pressured to consume. That is until college.

The first semester of college was met with a myriad of emotions for me. I was fearful of being away from home for the first time and awkwardly out of place in the social scene.

As I immersed myself into the college lifestyle, I noted a pattern: drinking. Crap, something I've avoided for years.

Luckily a friendly face from high school - whose name I cannot recall but face and laugh are forever engrained in my memory - shared the same dilemma as we found ourselves at our first college party.

In a dimly lit, crowded backyard with crappy acoustics and music, we both came up with a silly solution to fit in. We picked up an empty beer can, pretended to sip and acted like we were drunk.

We both couldn't stop laughing that others were buying it that we looked like the most wasted kids there. I don't think I've ever laughed harder.

Chapter 31: My first *real* drink

Spring semester I decided I needed a drink. Mom lost a breast. Dad seemed distant. And William appeared to be struggling in school.

Being merely 30-minutes away from my family created a barrier of which I could only do so much from afar. It was agonizing. My best friend was in pain, and I couldn't do a thing to make it better. I wasn't there.

As Valentine's Day approached, my friends and I experienced the loneliness all single women burden themselves with, surrounding this stupid manufactured day of love.

We knew it's a ploy for Hallmark to make a buck and the chocolate companies to contribute further to the nation's weight issue. Yet, we participated.

A group of beautiful, smart women got together at the ubiquitous Olive Garden to eat, gossip, laugh, reminisce and, for the first time ever, drink.

My first alcoholic drink was white wine which became my drink of choice until I realized I hate the headache that followed.

It's ironic as I write this memory I'm drinking a glass of white wine. No, I haven't converted. It's all I had available, and I'm lazy.

Chapter 32: A table of drinks *(present day)*

The four of us sat around a small round table in my hotel room. Each with a drink in hand, methodically taking sips to slowly ease the mind and temporarily forget the present.

As always, we drunkenly shared stories about mom. Stories about mom's difficulties with pumping gas were our trusty standbys.

Growing up mostly in Germany and in an age where gas attendants had a more hands on role, my mom didn't pump her own gas until she had to.

When I was 10, my mom asked me to put $10 on pump 87. Unknowingly, I darted into the gas station and asked the attendant as I was told. The woman laughed and said, "hon, we don't have 87 pumps." And she instructed me to go outside and ask my mom again.

"Mom, the gas attendant said that there are not 87 pumps. What's the pump number, mom?"

My mom, rarely one to get frustrated especially in public, looked around furiously for any other number on the pump. Not recognizing one turned to me and sternly yelled, "you go in there and tell her that it's pump 87 right now."

I did as I was told, and the response of the gas attendant is one I'll never forget. Laughing as she got on the intercom and in an authoritative voice states, "ma'am, please look for the large white number on the gas pump. What does it say?"

My mom, still unable to find the large white number, had to ask her gas pumping neighbor for help.

Stories like this made us laugh, grounded us and prepared us for what to face.

And this time, we also reminisced about Craig – from his ridiculous, high knee run to his impression of Jacque, a gay French tour guide Craig made up whenever we explored.

Craig's role in these drunken recounts was to provide commentary. Now he, too, was the subject as we drank and remembered those who left us too soon.

Chapter 33: Fool me once

Driving up the curvy roads to Virginia City, Craig listened intently to my stories of my college roommate and her romance comedy she was co-starring.

"We like to prank call the boy's dorm to find my crush we nicknamed Muppet Brow," I excitedly explained while taking both hands off the wheel to my brows and moving my fingers as if to showcase bushy eyebrows.

I went on to describe our quest to score Muppet Brow's phone number but resulted in Tina's future lover, Jim asking us to hang out. With no plans in our midst, other than to continue through the rolodex, we spent the evening bowling at a casino and eating at Awful Awful - a 24-hour greasy burger joint frequented by college kids and old men with gambling problems.

Tina and Jim fell instantly in love and it was the epitome of love at first sight. I will forever be grateful witnessing that love unfold before my eyes. To this day, they are still madly in love and have two beautiful children.

Craig listened quietly without much response or anything to contribute, which made me nervous. So,

I continued and shared funny drinking stories, that for most college students would seem benign.

Two weeks later, my mom and dad were yelling at me for drinking.

"How could you, Casey?" My dad sternly asked in disappointment and complete hypocrisy.

"But you're a Christian," my mom pleaded with tears in her eyes, realizing she didn't know everything about her daughter and best friend.

In effort to appear like the good kid, Craig shared my indiscretions with our folks.

Fool me once, shame on you. Fool me twice...well, fuck.

Chapter 34: Relay for life

In February 2002, we learned that my mom's cancer was terminal. She was given two-months to live.

At the time, I was dating Travis - a tiny, unassuming closeted gay man who I questioned daily about his sexuality. Travis was my first boyfriend. We dated nine-months, and we only kissed. Occasionally held hands.

I tried once to go further, and he wasn't hard. I was so innocent and ill-informed that I didn't take that as a blatant sign he is gay.

He is openly gay now and is no longer tiny. Living bicoastally as a model, Travis has blossomed into a beautifully, sculpted gay man.

I sometimes take photos of his shirtless, sometimes pant less Instagram photos, and send to my friend, Alise as a joke and reminder of the time I accused her of kissing Travis at an all-out jungle juice party we threw at our first apartment.

The UNR football team was in attendance, some kind of drug was being cooked on our stove, and the apartment was a mess. I lost my shit. That's what you get when you throw a party with a keg of jungle juice in the bathtub.

I decided to join them and after "catching" what I thought was Alise and Travis kissing in her bedroom.

To get revenge, I stripped off my clothes and sprinted down the street with a handful of other crazy drunk naked idiots.

After much counsel and drunken talk, I concluded that Travis and Alise were not messing around. It was just that Travis was just not into girls.

When I learned my mom was going not going to make it to my graduation or never see me get married, I called Travis to lean on my boyfriend for support.

He told me that he had plans to go to a fraternity party and then haphazardly asked me to come along.

I hung up the phone, wrote a note, gathered every item he ever gave me - his sister's old, ugly white faux leather purse, a purple feather boa and a zebra printed belt.

I walked his shit over and left it at the door. And never looked back.

Nine months of limp dick, questioning if he preferred men and lackluster support was enough for me to walk away.

After Travis, I started to mess around with the unconventionally cute Brent, a motocross enthusiast from Palmer, Alaska. Ironically, I shared a class with both Brent and Travis. I liked to play with fire.

As the summer hit, my mom started to fade. For some reason, she continued to clean houses as she lost weight and became more and more fragile.

She was stubborn, and after a weekend at a cabin loaned from Alise's family, my mom insisted in participating in the annual American Cancer Society's Relay for Life walk.

She walked the year before when she was in remission, had hair and vibrancy.

This year was different with a port, fluid in her lungs, opened wounds surrounding her chest - visible signs of the cancer that had now taken over her entire body.

Just weeks earlier she was in the hospital crying in agony as the doctor released the fluid from her lungs which was amassed by painful open wounds. It was agonizing to watch. I couldn't imagine the pain my mother endured. It breaks my heart every day thinking about it.

The Relay for Life event took place around my mom's birthday.

I had become painfully skinny, unable to eat due to the knowledge my mom was going to die and the thought of a new reality without my best friend.

My mom walked slightly bent over from the sharp pain she carried with every step around my high school track.

Each family member watched from a different part of the track, trying to mask their tears in an effort to support my mom.

I remember looking around at my family, one by one, each with the same stance - body quivering with arms wrapped around as if in a hug. I understood because I had the same pose.

And when mom neared each of us, we unwrapped our arms and started to clap, quickly found a second to wipe our tears and pretend we thought she had a fighting chance.

It was the last time she walked.

At 11pm that night, we had to rush mom to the hospital. She wasn't breathing.

Chapter 35: September 17

After the relay, mom was hospitalized for quite some time. Fluid had built up in her lungs to the point she couldn't breathe without assistance.

A new doctor assigned to our family gave us the hard truth. I appreciated him the most.

"Your mom has less than two weeks. Here's information about hospice care. I have already arranged someone to call you this afternoon with further details. I'm so sorry."

I stood stunned. My fears turned into a reality, and I couldn't find my feet. I somehow willed myself to my mom's side. She was sedated and unresponsive as I stroked her hands that looked like mine. I knew this was it.

I couldn't take much more and had to get out of the hospital, but I couldn't locate the exit and circled the white walled halls over and over, trying not to make eye contact. If I did, I knew I would crumble.

Once I found air, I fell to the ground and cried louder than I knew was possible. I felt alone.

After a couple of weeks with mom taking residence in the family room, I said my goodbyes. It was just after William's 10th birthday.

I looked over at my mom who was on so much morphine that she wasn't present and told her I loved her. And that it was okay to go.

I went on to share my favorite memories, which included our recent trip to San Francisco where we took a train from Reno, stayed in a Victorian style hotel, enjoyed a Russian Tea experience, laughed harder than we should have on tour of Alcatraz and shopped for the family.

It was one of my favorite memories not just with my mom but of my lifetime. A photo of that trip sits on my bookshelf at work. I look at it every day.

After a few hours, I got up and said my goodbyes. I had to go back to school and work – responsibility became my escapism.

I've never cried harder on the 30-mile stretch on the old 395 route to college. I felt empty.

The morning of September 17, I got up and looked at my calendar. "September 17," I said out loud to myself. "The day my mom dies."

Somehow, I willed myself to my classes throughout the day, barely eating a thing and perfunctorily engaging with classmates and friends.

I was easily convinced to skip class to escape a bit and go to a talk with Kyle from the Real-World Chicago season.

I sat front row center and listened to Kyle talk about his reality tv experience - one I was fascinated with - when I noticed Alise's sister, Brenda and our friends Tracey and Richie at the door. They looked concerned. I was motioned to come with them.

They told me what I already knew: my mom was gone.

Chapter 36: Fuck you, Tom

After my mom died, college became about how far I could push life.

I would drive the McCarran loop that traveled around Reno at 100 mph, praying I would die. Or at least get in an accident so I could feel numb.

I joined the girl's Rugby team and played girls twice my size at Berkeley, Stanford and UC Davis. I managed to play unscathed except for a time I knocked myself out cold by jumping on the quanco to avoid the other team from scoring.

I ran, climbed stairs and did sprints up and down the street, over and over, at midnight. Pounding the pavement so I couldn't hear my thoughts.

I drank to oblivion. I made out with strangers. I gave head to a few guys I just met.

I even made out with a hot UPS worker in my car after Alise jumped out of my moving vehicle due to a disagreement and picked up a pack of cigarettes.

For a week, we smoked in front of our apartment, but I never learned to inhale.

I was excessive, fearless and reckless. I guess I allowed myself time and space to heal - at least that is how I look back at it.

For my dad, he still had William, which he resented. He couldn't divulge. He couldn't be selfish. And he needed a release from the pain of watching a woman he was with for over 33 years take her last breath at 6:04pm.

But after a few years, William was older, and my dad could venture out. He was on the other side of his grieving and was ready to flirt with the concept of dating.

His idea of venturing out was Myspace and participating in every group chat that catered to women.

He was a busy man. In chat rooms, he was carrying on amusing narratives and conversations with a plethora of older women recently widowed, divorced or separated. But they all found God.

My dad took a liking to one sassy, intelligent woman named Sara from Tampa, Florida.

She was in her early 50's, recently divorced for the second time, had two adult children who still lived at home and short, stylish hair. She was the exact opposite of my mom - independent, witty, self-centered and a professional.

My dad flew to Tampa and felt instantly in lust. After meeting for the fifth time, my dad proposed after running smack into the bedroom sliding glass door with a cranberry vodka in hand.

Two months later, they got married on a boat.

I was invited yet I don't think I was wanted there. My dad avoided contact for the first two days I arrived in Tampa.

My response to his avoidance was to avoid my feelings and spend oodles of money on jet skis. It was worth the $800. I learned that chasing birds while jet skiing is one of the most cathartic things for me. Duly noted.

At the wedding, I realized my dad was on something. "Xanax," Sara proudly stated, "it will calm his nerves."

This was my second time meeting her in less than twenty-four hours. I got the sense she was controlling, and I immediately thought, "oh, you can only cage us for so long."

I sat in the back of the wedding ceremony, which was luckily outside, and I was able to shield my tears with sunglasses.

But the tears were relentless. I felt like I was watching my dad start a new life that I had zero room for me. I was losing another family member.

After the wedding, I barricaded myself into the boat's tiny bathroom only to be discovered by my new sisters who sympathetically asked if I wanted to be a part of the family photo. To that I chuckled, but obliged.

Sitting in the reception area, however, was too much for my soul to take. Looking around, I noted evidence of Sara and my dad's love. I saw photos of Sara's children. A few of William. And none of me. I felt left out in my father's new life.

The captain announced the boat was about to leave port and to welcome the happy couple, the bride and groom. At that moment, I looked over at Jack and firmly said, "we are getting off this boat."

We jumped off as the boat was leaving, clearing about a two-foot gap between the dock and the boat.

Six months after the wedding, my dad locked himself in the garage and kept his Jeep running. One of my sisters called the cops, and he was saved just in time.

By Florida law, my dad was placed in a mental institution for 72 hours.

And, so was Jack's father for trying to light his couch on fire. He was having withdrawals from alcohol and was hallucinating that there were ants surrounding the couch.

This is when Jack and I decided to marry remotely with as little to no family possible.

My dad and Sara divorced shortly after my dad was released. And, I coined the phrase, "Fuck you, Tom." Damn MySpace.

Chapter 37: The aftermath

My dad came out to visit after the divorce. He was a wreck.

Every night I came home from work, my father, eyes halfway open, would be sprawled out on the couch. He consumed a bottle of wine and several shots of whiskey a day.

After three weeks, I finally told him to leave.

He went back to our house in Carson City, which had been on the market since my dad moved to Florida to marry Sara.

The house was empty except for my dad's sleeping bag, and suitcase of clothes. He slept in William's old room, so no one could see the flashlight from the street. He also lost his mind.

One night I received a disturbing call from my dad. He obviously had been drinking but he sounded possessed.

I did have a feeling the house was haunted. The dryer would turn on by itself. Same with the microwave. And you always felt like you were being watched.

My dad, in a voice I've never heard before, told me how selfish I am, how he plans to drive to Florida and shoot Sara and then kill himself.

It was terrifying. He had been suicidal before. I just never was privy to the words inside his head.

I called Craig who lived down the street from my parent's house.

He drove over, and my dad refused to answer the door. But he did pick up the line. Craig was fed the same terrifying message and called the cops.

My dad mentioned he had a gun. Those magic words warranted a SWAT team. So, Craig was left with the decision to have our parent's house demolished to see if my dad's threats were real this time. Or, wait it out. He decided to wait it out.

And it wasn't until the next morning we knew my dad's fate. He signed onto Facebook and left a politically conservative comment.

At least we knew he was alive.

Chapter 38: A permanent residence

My dad picked up his life once again, as if the past never happened, and moved to Crystal River, Florida - a quirky, small town on the Gulf coast known for its manatees and the Three Sisters Springs.

My dad rented a space next to the Tiki bar and drank away his worries. William, now 14, lived with his biological dad for the first time in Carson. So, my dad was free to flail.

That is until he received a phone call from Craig. "William touched Sherry." That's enough to send William en route to my dad.

My dad was pissed but he moved into the larger place next to the Tiki bar and picked up raising William where he left off - with his right hand and short temper.

William and my dad found somewhat of a coexistence, learning how to avoid each other just enough to keep the peace.

William went through a number of phases while in Crystal River. From goth, to church goer, to one-girlfriend-kind-of-guy, to pot trier, to "too cool for school", to nerd. He barely graduated but graduated, and he decided to join the Army.

seventeen

He just wanted to get out of dodge for both the reputation my father carried and the one that he left behind.

Chapter 39: Broken dreams

Craig was at the top of his game at one point.

He purchased a beautiful home, had a thriving business, happy kids and a marriage.

But he couldn't maintain the lies. It all crumbled as the truth leaked out.

Craig had been cheating on Mindy with multiple woman, including minors.

Most of his indiscretions he could make up new lies to cover the truth. He even talked his way out of convictions. He was a smooth talker.

But this time he got caught. And no amount of lies could change Mindy's mind - she was fed up. This was it. She was done, and she divorced Craig.

After cops broke down the door to arrest Craig for child pornography to accusations from her friends claiming Craig made advances on their underage teenage daughters to the back taxes that went unpaid and bad business decisions that were made unilaterally, Craig slowly took down his own empire.

Chapter 40: Pulling the plug *(present day)*

Sitting in a small room outside the lobby with our nurse who I could tell had a compassionate heart and the representatives from the donor organization who just wanted Craig's organs, it dawned on me that this was it. Craig was gone.

Forty years on this planet, wreaking havoc with every relationship he maintained, business he worked and friendship he made. This was it.

As I listened to the next steps, a rundown of the paperwork my dad and I had to sign, I felt empty.

I wasn't mad at Craig. I forgave him.

I wasn't confused anymore. I understood him.

I was just sad.

I was losing another family member. And despite the fact that Craig caused me more pain than love, he was my blood. And my family was getting smaller.

I quickly bounced back into reality after learning that the process would be extended by a day, and that they would pull the plug in 48-hours.

I abruptly said "no, you will do it now. We have been through too much. You will do this today."

I walked out. And said my goodbyes to a man whom I both loved and hated.

Yet, I finally walked away.